The Ultimate Self-Teaching Method!

Level 1

🔊 o Access Included

Play Cello Today!

T0039676

To access audio visit:
www.halleonard.com/mylibrary

Enter Code
6936-5402-8884-8966

by Adrien Zitoun and Braden Zitoun
Cello recording by Adrien Zitoun
Audio Arrangements by Peter Deneff
Produced by Beat House Music

ISBN 978-1-4950-4593-6

HAL•LEONARD®
CORPORATION
7777 W. BLUEMOUND RD. P.O. BOX 13819 MILWAUKEE, WI 53213

In Australia Contact:
Hal Leonard Australia Pty. Ltd.
4 Lentara Court
Cheltenham, Victoria, 3192 Australia
Email: ausadmin@halleonard.com.au

Visit Hal Leonard Online at
www.halleonard.com

The Basics

The Cello

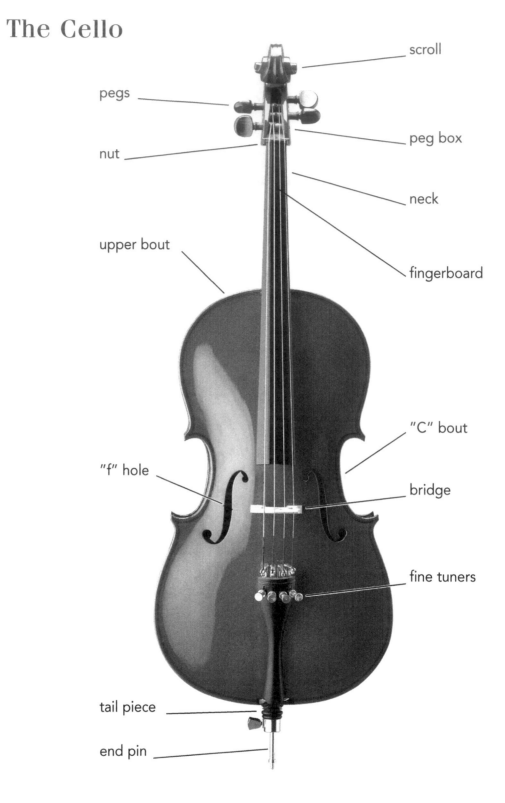

- scroll
- pegs
- peg box
- nut
- neck
- upper bout
- fingerboard
- "C" bout
- "f" hole
- bridge
- fine tuners
- tail piece
- end pin

The Bow

- adjusting screw
- stick
- winding
- tip
- bow hair
- ferrule
- frog

Sitting with the Cello

The Chair

Because we sit while we play the cello, the chair is a very important component to proper position and posture. You will need an armless chair or stool that has a flat sitting surface and does not tilt backwards. The height of the chair will vary depending on the height of the player. Your knees should not be higher than your hips.

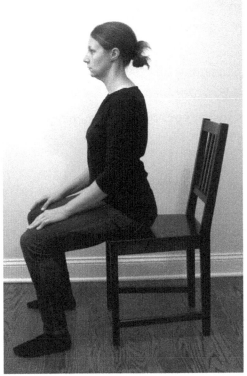

Length of Endpin

The length of your endpin depends on your height and the height of the chair. When standing up with the cello, the scroll should not be higher than your eyes. Another way to determine the length is to sit without the endpin out. Holding the cello between your knees and at your sternum, slowly let out the endpin until it touches the floor. You may need a helper for this.

Posture

Sitting properly is crucial to holding the cello correctly and producing the best sound. Sit at the front edge of the chair. Your feet should be flat, facing forward and directly below your knees. Make sure that your back is straight and that you are sitting tall. Your knees should be on the sides of the cello, holding the cello in place. The cello will hit in the middle of the chest, at the sternum. Bring the cello into the body,

keeping your back straight, or slightly forward toward the cello. Make sure that you do not tilt back. The pegs will slip in right behind the left side of your neck. Be sure to keep your head tall and straight. It may take a while to find the ideal posture and placement of your cello. Experiment until you are comfortable and relaxed.

Preparing Your Bow

When a bow is stored in its case, the hair is loosened. After taking the bow from your case to play, you will need to tighten the hair by turning the screw clockwise, until the hair is straight and firm, still leaving the stick visibly bowed. Take care not to over-tighten the hair, which could damage the bow.

Before playing, rosin the bow by sliding the hair back and forth across the rosin. You can apply a little rosin each time you take your bow out to play.

Remember to loosen the bow hair by turning the screw counterclockwise before putting the bow back in the case again.

Holding the Bow

Holding the bow properly is just as important as correctly holding the cello. As you learn to hold the bow for the first time, put down your cello so your left hand can assist you. As you become more comfortable with your bow, you will be able to pick it up easily with your right hand alone.

Start by placing the bow on your lap, with the frog on the right, and the hair facing out. You should always avoid touching the hair. Next, put the pad of your right middle finger on the ferrule of the bow, making sure that your fingers are flat, and not curved. The other fingers should be evenly spaced, with the ring and pinky fingers on the frog of the bow, and the index finger gently resting on the winding.

After these four fingers are in position, lift the bow up vertically using your left hand, without disturbing the placed fingers. Place the tip of your right thumb where the left end of the frog

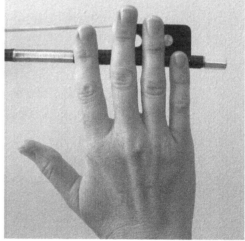

meets the stick. Keep the thumb loosely bent. Your hand should be relaxed with the fingers spread comfortably. You will need to practice finding this position several times each day until it becomes easy.

Learning to hold the bow properly takes patience and practice. As you begin to learn notes on the cello, you may wish to pluck the strings first, instead of using the bow right away. Plucking a stringed instrument is called *pizzicato*. As you play new notes and pieces *pizzicato*, continue to practice holding the bow to become more comfortable with it.

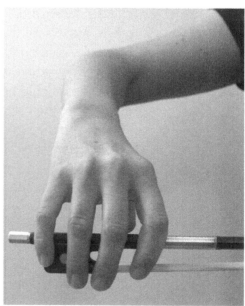

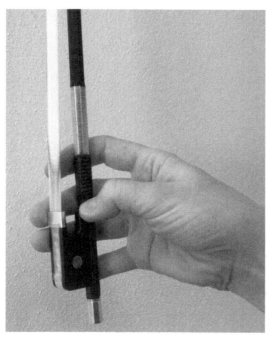

Tuning Your Cello

The four strings on the cello are tuned to the following pitches, from bottom (low) to top (high): C, G, D, A

The majority of tuning is done with the fine tuners. Use of the pegs is reserved for larger adjustments in pitch (usually more than a whole step). Turning the fine tuners clockwise, or tightening them, raises the pitch, while turning them counterclockwise, or loosening them, lowers the pitch. Until you are more comfortable holding your bow, it might be easier to tune by plucking each string.

Tune your A string first by listening to the A tone on the audio track. You can also use the A pitch from a keyboard or tuner. Listen to the pitch, and adjust the string as necessary to match it. If your A string sounds lower than the A that you are matching, slowly turn the A string fine tuner clockwise. This will tighten the string and make the pitch higher. If your A is higher than the A tone you are matching, loosen the string by turning the fine tuner counterclockwise. When your A string is in tune, continue with the other strings, working your way down to the C string.

If your cello is so out of tune that the fine tuners cannot reach the desired pitch, you will need to do the bulk of the tuning with the pegs, and then finish the small adjustments with the fine tuners.

Tuning Tips

Because of the conical shape of the pegs, make sure that if you have to use them, push in at the same time that you are turning—otherwise the peg will not stay put and the pitch will slowly go down.

While tightening or loosening a string, turn the peg slowly, especially when tuning to a higher pitch. The string could break if stretched too much. Go slow and check often!

Maintenance and Accessories

To keep your cello and bow in good condition, you will need a case. You will need rosin for your bow, and a soft cloth for removing fingerprints and rosin dust before putting your cello back in the case. When cleaning the bow, you should wipe the stick, but not the bow hair. To protect the wood of the instrument from cracking, use a cello humidifier during cold or dry months of the year. The use of an endpin holder, or "rock stop" is highly recommended to help keep the cello from sliding on the floor while playing. There are various kinds of endpin holders, from straps to discs. You may wish to experiment with several types to decide what works best for you.

Reading Music

Musical sounds are indicated by symbols called **notes**. The two most important components to every note are pitch and rhythm.

Pitch

Pitch (the highness or lowness of a note) is indicated by the vertical placement of a note on the staff. Notes higher on the staff are higher in pitch, and notes lower on the staff are lower in pitch. To name the pitches, we use the first seven letters of the alphabet: A, B, C, D, E, F, and G. The **bass clef** (𝄢) assigns a particular pitch name to each line and space on the staff, centered around the pitch F, located on the second line from the top. 𝄢

While most cello music is written in bass clef, it is also common to see music in a higher register written in tenor, or even treble clef. To begin with, you will work only with bass clef.

C D E F G A B C D E F G A B C D

To remember the line names easily, use the acronym **G**reat **B**ig **D**olphin **F**ins, and for the spaces, spell **FACE**.

Great   Big   Dolphin   Fins

Rhythm

Rhythm refers to the elements of time—how long, or for how many beats a note lasts, including spaces or rests in between notes. Notes of different durations are represented by the following symbols:

| whole note | dotted half note | half note | quarter note |
| (four beats) | (three beats) | (two beats) | (one beat) |

To help you keep track of beats in a piece of music, the staff is divided into **measures** (or **bars**). A **time signature** at the beginning of the staff indicates how many beats you can expect to find in each measure.

Time signature   bar line   measure

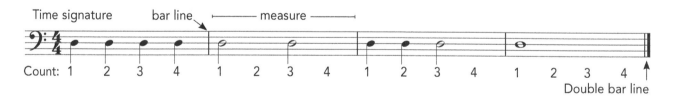

Count: 1 2 3 4   1 2 3 4   1 2 3 4   1 2 3 4
                                                      Double bar line

$\frac{4}{4}$ is perhaps the most common time signature. The top number indicates how many beats there are in each measure. The bottom number shows what kind of note value receives one beat. (The number 4 is most often on the bottom, but numbers such as 8 or even 2 are used as well.) In $\frac{4}{4}$ time, there are four beats in each measure, and each beat is worth one quarter note.

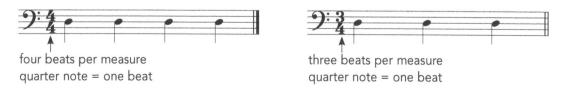

four beats per measure   three beats per measure
quarter note = one beat   quarter note = one beat

Open Strings

From lowest to highest, the cello strings are: C G D A

Memorize the names of the strings and their corresponding notes on the staff. Begin without your bow and play the notes *pizzicato* (*pizz.*). *Pizzicato* is an Italian word, which means "to pluck."

With your cello in proper playing position, rest your right thumb against the lower right-hand edge of the fingerboard. Use your middle finger to pluck each open string. As you pluck each string, starting from the lowest string, say the note name while looking at its position on the staff. A gentle but assertive plucking motion is the key to a pleasant tone.

Be careful not to pluck so hard that the string snaps against the fingerboard.

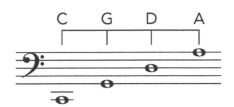

Pizzicato vs. Arco

There are two options for producing sound: *pizzicato* (plucking), and *arco* (with the bow). The term *arco* is usually used to instruct the player to start using the bow after a passage that was just played *pizzicato*. When no indication is given, you will use the bow (*arco*).

Note Names

Say the names of the open strings aloud as you play "Open String Pizzicato" and "Open String Challenge." Pay close attention to the note's position on the staff. You can do this until you feel comfortable reading all the notes.

Open String Pizzicato

Track 2

Open String Challenge

Track 3

Using the Bow

Sit with your cello in its proper playing position. Because this exercise does not involve fingered notes (left hand), rest your hand on your left knee. Holding your bow correctly, place the hair on the D string, starting near the frog, about halfway between the bridge and the end of the fingerboard. Try to keep the bow hair flat as you draw the bow across the string. The bow should always be perpendicular to the string that you are playing on. Draw the bow across the string, opening your arm from the shoulder in a horizontal motion to the right. This is called a **down bow** (⊓). The first half of a down bow mostly opens from the shoulder, and the second half of the down bow mostly opens from the elbow.

The opposite motion (from tip to frog) is called an **up bow** (∨). Starting at the tip of the bow, push the bow towards the frog. The first half of the up bow mostly closes from the elbow and the second half of an up bow mostly closes from the shoulder.

In order to sustain the sound, you will also need to adjust the height of your elbow. As you travel toward the tip, your elbow should gradually get higher, transferring the weight of your arm into your index finger. As you come back on an up bow, bring your elbow back to its original position.

Practice bowing each open string to become comfortable with the down bow and up bow motions. When playing on the A string, the arm will be higher, in order to avoid hitting the D string. When playing on the C string, your arm should adjust to a lower height, following the curve of the bridge. If you become tense or tired while playing, stop and rest a few moments before you resume. Try to feel the natural weight of the arm rather than pressing.

> **Down bow** (⊓) – Drawing the bow to the right
>
> **Up bow** (∨) – Drawing the bow to the left

As you play "Open String Bowing," use a down bow for the first half note in each measure, and an up bow for the second half note in each measure.

Track 4

Open String Bowing

Keep your bow halfway between the bridge and the end of the fingerboard. Your arm height will adjust depending on what string you are playing. Be careful not to raise your shoulders.

Track 5

More Open Strings

Practice checklist:

- Proper cello position
- Relaxed bow hold
- Bow placed halfway between bridge and fingerboard
- Slight arm height adjustment from string to string
- Steady quarter note beat
- Memorize open string note names

"Open String Warm-up" can be used as a daily warm-up. Play it *pizzicato* first, and then use your bow.

Track 6

Open String Warm Up

repeat sign

The two dots next to the double bar line at the end of the song are a **repeat sign**, meaning to go back to the beginning of the song and play it a second time.

Notes on the D String

New Note: E

The note E sounds a whole step above the open D string. Place your 1st finger on the D string about 3 inches below the nut to sound the note E. Keep your other fingers curved and hovering over the string, but not touching the string. Be careful not to let your fingers curl into your palm.

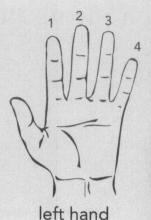

left hand

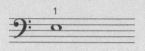

The diagram above shows each finger with an assigned number. It's important to learn the finger number that is associated with playing a certain note. Sometimes you'll see small finger numbers above the notes in your music examples. These numbers serve as a further guide for playing the correct note with the proper finger.

Left Hand and Arm Position

When fingering notes with your left hand, make sure that your thumb is near the center of the neck, and opposite your 2nd finger. Your elbow should be high and your wrist flat. Having rounded fingers (almost like a "C" shape) will ensure that you are applying proper weight to the string. To find the correct elbow height, extend your left arm out completely at shoulder level. Gradually close your elbow to bring your hand back to the cello, without lowering your elbow.

Intervals

A **scale** consists of whole step and half step intervals. An **interval** is the distance between two pitches.

Whole Step: A whole step is an interval that consists of two half steps.

Half Step: A half step is the smallest distance between two notes.

Concentrate on keeping your 1st finger round, and your elbow high in "1st Finger on D String."

1st Finger on D String

As you play "Aiming for E" (*pizzicato*), concentrate on the sound of the whole step between open D string and first finger E. Determine exactly where to place your 1st finger to sound a whole step higher.

Track 9

Aiming for E

New Note: F♯

F♯ sounds a whole step higher than 1st finger E. To play F♯, place your 3rd finger about 2 ½ inches from the 1st finger, keeping your 1st and 2nd fingers on the D string. Remember, your thumb should be opposite your 2nd finger.

Track 10

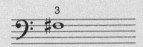

Memorize where the 1st and 3rd fingers are placed to sound the E and F♯. To improve your **intonation**, or accuracy of pitch, use a combination of your ear and the online audio. You can also match pitches using a keyboard or digital tuner.

3rd Finger on D String

Track 11

As you play "Putting It All Together," pluck the notes slowly, concentrating on finger placement and intonation. Increase the **tempo** (speed) as you get more comfortable. When the notes become easy, use the bowings given, but start slowly at first. Notice that in the fourth measure, we go from D up to F♯, skipping E. When playing the F♯, fingers 1, 2, and 3 will go down on the string at the same time.

Putting It All Together

Track 12

Three Finger Rhythm Challenge

Track 13

Hot Cross Buns

Track 14

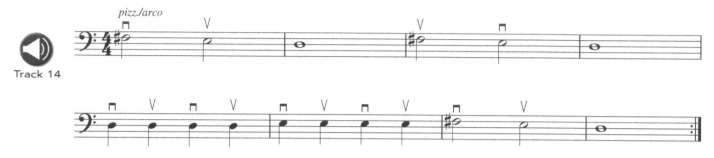

Rests

Rests are symbols that indicate beats of silence.

> **Quarter Rest** = 1 beat of silence – the same duration as a quarter note.
>
> **Half Rest** = 2 beats of silence – the same duration as a half note.
>
> **Whole Rest** = 4 beats of silence – the same duration as a whole note, or simply resting for a whole measure.

| quarter rest (one beat) | half rest (two beats) | whole rest (four beats or one whole measure) |

Resting Song

Track 15

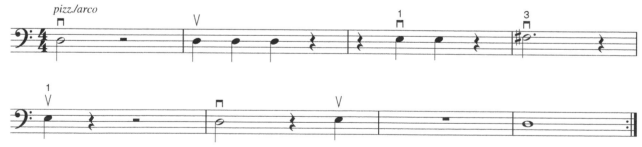

"Mary's Little Lamb" uses D, E, and F♯. Make sure to observe the quarter-note rests.

Mary's Little Lamb

Track 16

New Note: G

Track 17

The note G sounds a half step above the 3rd finger F♯. This is a smaller interval than the whole steps you have been playing. Place your 4th finger about 1¼ inches from your 3rd finger. Keep fingers 1, 2, and 3 down on the D string while you play your 4th finger. Remember to keep your thumb opposite your 2nd finger. Be sure that your left elbow is up and that your fingers are rounded.

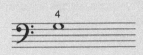

New Note G

Track 18

Practice "D String Etude" *pizzicato* first. As you approach the 4th finger G, keep the other fingers down on the string. Do not squeeze your thumb.

D String Etude

Track 19

"Bile 'em Cabbage" is a popular American fiddle tune. Keep a steady quarter-note beat using smooth long bows for the half notes.

Bile 'em Cabbage

Track 20

Notes on the A String

Before we move over to the A string and learn some new notes, use "Open String Review" to refresh your memory on the note names. You may also use this as an opportunity to practice slightly lowering and raising your bow arm as you move from string to string to play each note clearly.

Open String Review

Track 21

New Note: B

Track 22

The note B sounds a whole step higher than the open A string. It's played with your 1st finger, and is found about 3 inches below the nut, in the same place as your 1st finger on the D string.

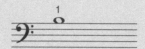

Whole Step Happiness

Track 23

Whole Step Hoedown

Track 24

New Note: C♯

Track 25

The note C♯ sounds a whole step higher than 1st finger B. Place your 3rd finger on the A string about 2 ½ inches from the 1st finger, letting finger 4 hover gently over the fingerboard. Remember to keep the 1st and 2nd fingers down on the string while playing finger 3.

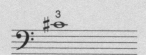

Putting It Together on the A String

Track 26

Take a minute to check for a relaxed bow hold, a high left elbow, low shoulders, and rounded fingers.

Hot Cross Buns in A

Track 27

Mary's Little Lamb in A

Track 28

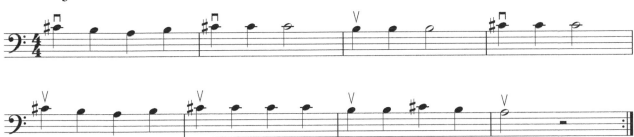

D Major Key Signature

A **key signature** indicates what notes to play sharp (♯) or flat (♭) throughout an entire piece. When sharps or flats are in the key signature, they no longer need to appear next to the notes on the staff. Instead, you'll find the sharps or flats at the beginning of each line of music. A key signature with two sharps indicates that all written Fs and Cs should be played as sharps. This is the **Key of D**.

Lift and Breathe

The **comma** above the staff (') in "French Folk Song" is a sign to lift the bow. This is the same symbol used to tell wind players to take a breath. This lift motion is also referred to as a **circle bow**, since you are making a circle in the air, and returning the bow to the starting point for another down bow. As a string player, it's good to use these markings not only to lift the bow, but to breathe as well. Doing so helps promote a kind of natural phrasing to the song you are playing.

Now try "French Folk Song." When playing *arco*, notice that each measure begins down bow (⊓). In measure 4, lift your bow during the half rest so you can begin down bow (⊓) again in measure 5.

French Folk Song

Track 29

Play C# as indicated by the key signature.

New Note: D

Track 30

The note D sounds a half step higher than 3rd finger C#. To play a D on the A string, place your 4th finger about 1 ¼ inches from your 3rd finger, leaving fingers 1, 2, and 3 down on the fingerboard. This D is an octave higher than the open D string. To compare the sound, play open D and then D on the A string.

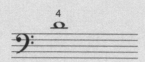

A String Etude

Track 31

Notice the time signature in "Melody." There are three beats in each measure. Use a longer bow stroke to give the dotted half note three full beats.

Melody

Track 32

4th Finger Fitness

Track 33

Playing on the D and A Strings

Lesson 5

Now that you have learned the notes on the D and A strings, you are ready to play a song that uses both strings. Remember to think about the height of your right elbow as you change strings, as well as keeping your bow in between the bridge and the end of the fingerboard.

"Jingle Bells" uses notes on the D string along with the open A string. Notice the lift in measures 4 and 12. Practice this counterclockwise motion in the air before putting your bow on the string.

Track 34

Jingle Bells

Playing the D Major Scale

You are now ready to play a D Major scale. A **scale** is a series of ascending or descending notes, arranged sequentially (following the alphabet, in order). The type of scale is defined by the intervals between each note, primarily by which are half steps (**H**) or whole steps (**W**). For example, the arrangement of **W W H W W W H** is a **major scale**. To begin on D and follow this pattern would give us: D E F♯ G A B C♯ D. Starting with the open D string, play up to finger 4; the note G. Continue, now starting on the open A string, going up to finger 4, sounding the note D (an octave higher than where you started).

Play the scale *pizzicato* with the online audio to check for intonation. Play the scale *arco* when the fingering becomes easy.

Track 35

D Major Scale

In "Aunt Rhody," concentrate on your bow lengths. Try to use twice as much bow on the half notes as on the quarter notes. However, it's not necessary to use the entire bow length for the half notes.

Aunt Rhody

Intervals

An **interval** is the distance between two pitches. So far, we have discussed the intervals half step and whole step. Your cello is tuned by another interval, the fifth. From bottom to top, each string is a fifth apart: **C** (d e f) **G** (a b c) **D** (e f g) **A**. To find any interval, count, beginning with the first pitch as one, and stop at the desired pitch. This number is the interval. For example, A up to C is a third: A (1), B (2), C (3), = third.

For the following well-known folk tune, notice the use of the fifth, between the open D and A strings. Also notice the use of descending D Major scale segments.

Twinkle, Twinkle Little Star

In the next music example, the theme from Dvorak's "New World Symphony," notice the line marked over the notes in measures 1-2, 3, and 5-6. This is a reminder that after playing 3rd finger on F♯, you should keep this finger on the D string while you play open A, since you will be coming right back to the same F♯. In order to keep 3 down and not touch the open A string, you will need to make a "tunnel" with high, rounded fingers.

New World Symphony Theme

Dvořák

Notes on the G String

New Note: A

The A sounds a whole step above the open G string. Place your 1st finger on the G string about 3 inches from the nut to sound A. This is an octave below the open A string. Remember to keep your other fingers hovering over the fingerboard.

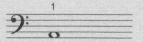

As you learn the G string notes, observe that your left elbow is higher than when you are playing on the D and A strings. Your thumb should continue to remain soft, and opposite your 2nd finger.

A New Note

Track 40

New Note: B

Track 41

The B sounds a whole step higher than A. Place your 3rd finger on the G string about 2 ½ inches from your 1st finger to sound B. Remember to keep your 1st and 2nd fingers down when you play your 3rd finger.

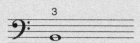

As you play "Whole Step Waltz," listen for whole steps between open G, A, and B. Check the time signature. How many beats are in each measure?

Whole Step Waltz

Track 42

20

Track 43

Hot Cross Buns in G

Upbeat

An **upbeat**, also called a "pick-up note," is a note or notes that appear before a **downbeat**, or first beat, of a measure. When this happens at the beginning of a song, the missing beats are often found at the end of the song.

Track 44

Oh Susannah

Track 45

New Note: C

The note C is a half step higher than B. Place your 4th finger on the G string, about 1 ¼ inches from the 3rd finger to sound C. Your 4th finger C on the G string is an octave above your open C string. Remember to leave all of your fingers down when playing C.

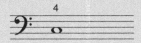

Close Friends

Track 46

Playing the G Major Scale

You are now ready to play a G Major scale. If you use the same pattern of whole and half steps as you did in the D Major scale (**W W H W W W H**), you would begin on the open G string and follow this pattern to end with 4th finger on the D string. This pattern uses an F♯.

G Major Scale

Track 47

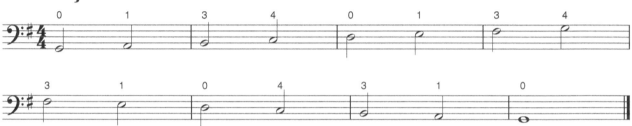

"Hungarian Folk Song" uses notes on both the D and G strings. Play slowly at first, and when you are comfortable with the notes and rhythms, try a livelier tempo.

Hungarian Folk Song

Track 48

Bartok

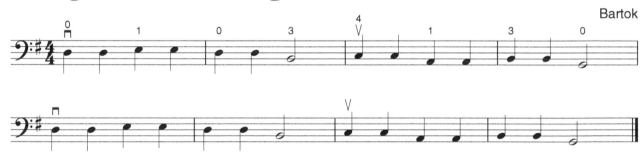

While you play "Long, Long Ago," pay attention to your bow divisions. Make sure that you travel far enough toward the upper half of the bow before the whole notes, so you don't get stuck at the frog before finishing the full value of the note.

Long, Long Ago

Now try "Twinkle, Twinkle Little Star" in the key of G. Take a moment to double check your bow hand, your sitting position, and your left arm and hand. Make sure that you are not squeezing the neck of the cello with your thumb.

Twinkle, Twinkle Little Star

Notes on the C String

Track 51

New Note: D
The note D sounds a whole step higher than the open C string. Place your 1st finger on the C string about 3 inches below the nut to sound D. This D is one octave below the open D string. Remember to check the height of your elbow, and make sure that your other fingers are hovering over the C string.

While playing "C String Serenade," focus on your bow, making sure that it is parallel to the bridge. Use the weight of your arm to produce the sound. Do not squeeze the bow.

Track 52

C String Serenade

Track 53

New Note: E
The note E sounds a whole step higher than D. Place your 3rd finger on the C string about 2 ½ inches from the 1st finger to sound E. Remember to leave your 1st finger down on the D when playing this note.

In "Wonderful Waltz," notice the time signature. How many beats are there in each measure?

Track 54

Wonderful Waltz

In "Low Notes Etude" you will play notes on both the G and C strings.

Low Notes Etude

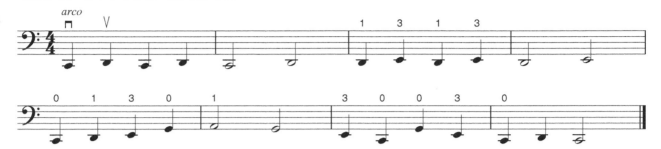

New Note: F

The note F sounds a half step higher than E. Place your 4th finger on the C string, about 1 ¼ inches from the 3rd finger to sound F.

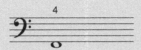

Old French Tune

Frère Jacques

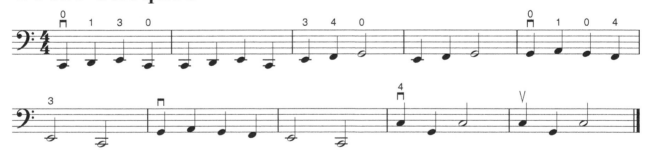

Tempo Markings

Tempo refers to the speed at which a piece of music is played. In music, tempo markings are often Italian. A few common tempo markings include:

Allegro: fast

Moderato: moderate

Andante: slower "walking" tempo

Largo: very slow

The beautiful "Scottish Air," also known as "Annie Laurie," presents you with a new bowing challenge. Notice in measure 2 there are two up bows marked in a row (V V). Here you will need to stop your bow in between the notes, but continue in the same up bow direction. This is also called a "hooked" bow stroke. Make sure to save enough bow for the second note. This bowing pattern is found in measures 2, 6, and 14. Practice these measures separately to get a feel for this new bowing. Don't forget to begin the piece with an up bow on the first pick-up note.

Track 59

Scottish Air

The Octave

You have already learned the intervals half step, whole step, and fifth. Another important interval makes an appearance in "Scottish Air." The **octave** is the distance from one letter name, to the nearest note of the same letter name, i.e., C to the next C up or down. In "Scottish Air," octaves appear in measures 1, 5, and 15. Watch carefully for octaves in all songs, and make sure that you play them in tune.

2nd Finger

Up until now you have played fingers 1, 3, and 4 in just about the same place on each string. Although you were putting your 2nd finger down along with fingers 3 and 4, we did not learn these note names. In this lesson, we will start playing notes with the 2nd finger.

New Note: F

The note F sounds a half step higher than E. Place your 2nd finger on the D string, about 1 ¼ inches from the 1st finger to sound F. Remember to leave the 1st finger down on the string as well.

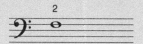

2nd Finger Lament

Andante

Minor vs. Major

So far, we have played songs in a **major** key. In general, major keys sound happy and bright. **Minor** keys sound sad and dark. Whether a song is in major or minor depends largely on where the half steps are positioned in the scale.

Try "Sad Aunt Rhody" playing all the F♯'s as F♮, with finger 2 instead of finger 3. Playing the F♯ puts "Aunt Rhody" in a major key, while playing F♮ changes "Aunt Rhody" to a minor key.

Sad Aunt Rhody

Slowly

New Note: C

The note C sounds a half step higher than B. Place your 2nd finger on the A string, about 1 ¼ inches from the 1st finger to sound C. Make sure your thumb is opposite your 2nd finger.

Track 63

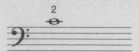

Track 64

Close Friends

Moderato

Track 65

German Folk Song

Moderately fast

"Folk Song" uses 2nd finger on both the D and A strings. Notice the absence of sharps in the key signature.

Track 66

Folk Song

Allegro

28

Are you ready for a challenge? "Bingo" uses C♮ (2nd finger on the A string) and F♯ (3rd finger on the D string). Also, remember to leave your 1st finger down in measures 4 and 5, and your 4th finger down in measures 9 and 10. This will only work if your fingers are rounded.

Bingo

Track 67

Moderato

Playing finger 2 on the D string does not always mean that you are playing in a minor key. In the example below, "Merry Widow," you will play 2nd finger, but will be in the key of C Major. Be aware of the bow lift in measure 24.

Merry Widow

Track 68

Moderate Waltz

Two-Octave C Scale

Track 69

Now that you have learned 2nd finger on the D and A strings, you are ready to learn your first two-octave scale. You will start on the open C string, and play 15 consecutive notes up to 2nd finger on the A string. Be aware that you will be using 2nd finger on the D and A strings, but 3rd finger on the C and G strings.

Andante

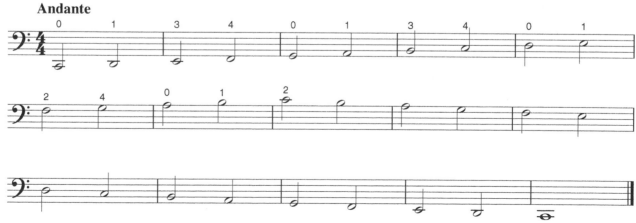

Eighth Notes

An **eighth note** equals one half the value of a quarter note. Eighth notes often appear in music in groups of two or four notes beamed together. Two eighth notes equal the value of one quarter note.

Counting

You may wish to practice counting eighth notes without your cello at first. You can clap the quarter note beat with your hands and speak the eighth note rhythm, or vice versa. Setting your metronome to a steady quarter note beat and clapping or speaking the rhythm is also a very good practice technique.

Play the one octave D Major scale below using eighth note rhythms. Set a quarter note beat to determine the speed of your eighth notes. Once you are comfortable with clapping the rhythms, use your bow. Pay close attention not to use the same amount of bow for the eighth notes as you do the quarter notes.

Track 70

Eighth Notes

Track 71

Lightly Row

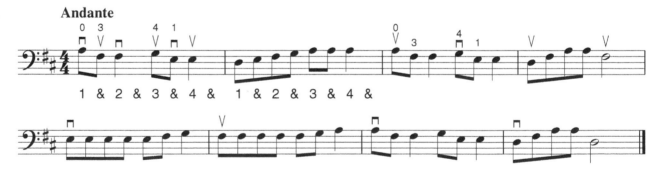

Track 72

Slurs and Legato

String players often slur notes together. A **slur** is a curved line that connects notes that are different in pitch. Notes connected by a slur are played in the same bow stroke. Playing multiple notes in one bow stroke will cause the notes to sound smooth and connected. This style is known as **legato**.

In this next song, "Plenty to Slur," practice not stopping your bow in between the two notes under the slur. Your bow should continue to move at an even speed for both notes.

Track 73

Plenty to Slur

Observe the Music

A helpful tip to aid in learning any piece of music is to spend some time looking over the music before ever playing a note. Look for anything tricky that may come up: large interval skips, 2nd vs. 3rd finger, slurs, bow divisions, or even change in key or meter. It is also useful to look for repeated patterns within the music. Some measures may look like something that occurred earlier, but in fact might be slightly different. Recognizing anything new or tricky will help you prepare to play the song.

"Country Gardens" contains many repeated patterns. Identifying these will help you to learn the piece more quickly. Make sure you are observing the slurs and eighth-note patterns. Since these elements are rather new, go slowly. It might be a good idea to clap the rhythm before playing with the cello.

Track 74

Country Gardens

D.C. al Fine

D.C. stands for *Da Capo*, which means "to the beginning" in Italian. *Fine* means "end." When you see this sign, go back to the beginning of the song and play until *Fine*.

Track 75

Caribbean Folk Song

Practice Tips

"Caribbean Folk Song" is lively and fun to play. Some useful practice tips may include:

- Look over the music before playing, noticing every mark and symbol
- Clap or speak the rhythm
- Play pizzicato first to become familiar with the notes
- Be aware of slurred notes

Tie

A **tie** is a musical symbol shaped as a curved line, which connects two notes of the same pitch. Notes connected by a tie are played as one single note. Many ties are used to extend notes beyond the bar line. As you look through "Amazing Grace" you will notice a tie in measures 7 and 8. The dotted half note (three beats) tied to a half note (two beats) will be held for five beats.

Be careful not to confuse a tie with a slur. A slur connects different notes under the same bow. A tie holds the same note longer, without a bow change.

Track 76

Amazing Grace

Dynamics

Dynamics indicate how loud or soft the music will be played. Traditionally, dynamic terms are known by their Italian names.

p	piano	soft	*mp*	mezzo piano	moderately soft
f	forte	loud	*mf*	mezzo forte	moderately loud

Using a heavier bow stroke and a faster bow speed will create a louder tone. A slower bow speed and less weight will create a softer tone.

In "Spring from The Four Seasons," notice that your 4th finger will have to move quickly from the D string to the A string. In these measures you will need to make sure that your 4th finger is in place before you move the bow. Also notice the dynamic change to *p* in measure 6. Use less bow to produce a softer sound.

Track 77

Spring from The Four Seasons

Vivaldi

Think about your bow divisions in "Musette." Travel to the upper half of the bow for the first half note, and stay there for the four eighth notes. In measure 2, travel back to the lower half of the bow, and stay there for the next four eighth notes.

Track 78

Musette

J.S. Bach

Crescendo and Decrescendo (or Diminuendo)

There are two musical terms that indicate a gradual change in dynamics. **Crescendo** means to gradually get louder. **Decrescendo** means to gradually get softer. Symbols represent these terms to make it easy to see where, and for how long the change in dynamic should occur.

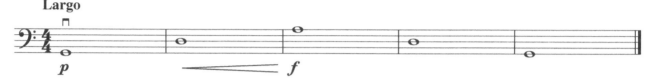

crescendo (cresc.)

decrescendo, or diminuendo (decresc. or dim.)

Practice *crescendo* and *decrescendo* as you play the following open string exercises. Pay attention to the weight and bow speed adjustments needed to create the sound you desire. Remember to gradually adjust the height of your elbow so you feel the weight in your index finger as you travel toward the tip of the bow.

Open String Crescendo

Track 79

Largo

Open String Decrescendo

Track 80

Andante

Because *forte* sounds are easier to play near the frog of the bow, long-note decrescendos are often played starting on a down bow. Crescendos are more easily executed with an up bow. Though this bowing is common, the reverse is still possible, and sometimes unavoidable.

With "Open String Shading" practice opening and closing your elbow with each long bow stroke. Remember, when you are starting at the tip, the first half of the up bow closes from the elbow, and the second half closes from the shoulder. The opposite will be true starting on a down bow. Concentrate on not squeezing your thumb, and keeping your shoulders low and relaxed.

Open String Shading

Track 81

Freely

In "Scarborough Fair," words are used to indicate *crescendo* and *decrescendo* instead of symbols. The *crescendo* starts in measure 5, and continues until the *forte* in measure 9. The same applies to the decrescendo found in measure 13. Practice these measures until your dynamic shadings are smooth and easy.

Track 82

Scarborough Fair

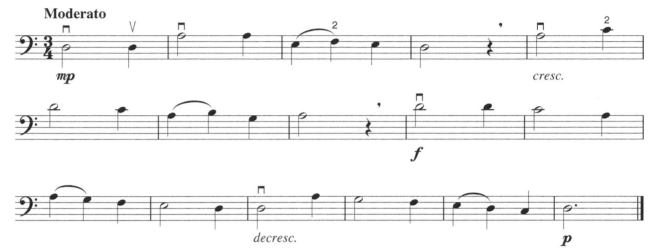

Let's put everything you've learned together in the next two duets. With "When the Saints Go Marching In" and "Boatman Dance," you have a chance to find someone who also knows how to play the cello, and practice playing with another live musician. You will play the cello 1 part, and your partner will play cello 2. Listen to each other! You may play along with the audio, or together without the track.

When the Saints Go Marching In (Duet)

Boatman Dance (Duet)

Track 85

Track 86

36

Fingering Chart

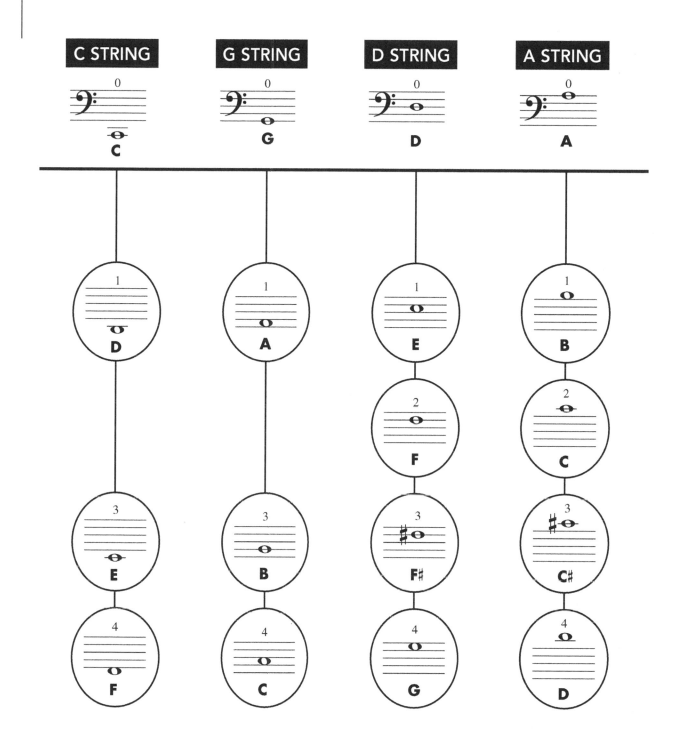

Glossary of Musical Terms

Accent (>)	An Accent mark (>) means to emphasize the note to which it is attached.
Accidental	Any sharp (♯), flat (♭), or natural (♮) sign that appears in the music but is not in the key signature.
Allegro	Fast tempo.
Andante	Slower "walking" tempo.
Arco	With the bow.
Bass Clef (𝄢)	(F Clef) indicates the position of note names on a music staff. The fourth line in bass clef is F.
Bar Lines	Bar Lines divide the music staff into measures.
Beat	The pulse of music, like a heartbeat, should remain very steady. Counting aloud and foot-tapping help maintain a steady beat.
Breath Mark	The Breath Mark (') indicates a specific place to inhale or, on a string instrument, a place to lift the bow.
Chord	When two or more notes are played together, they form a chord or harmony.
Chromatic Notes	Chromatic Notes are altered with sharps, flats and natural signs which are not in the key signature.
Chromatic Scale	The smallest distance between two notes is a half step, and a scale made up of consecutive half steps is called a Chromatic Scale.
Common Time	Common Time (𝄴) is the same as $\frac{4}{4}$ time signature.
Crescendo	Play gradually louder. (*cresc.*)
D.C. al Fine	Play again from the beginning, stopping at Fine. D.C. is the abbreviation for Da Capo, or "to the beginning," and Fine means "the end."
Decrescendo	Play gradually softer. (*decresc.*)
Diminuendo	Same as decrescendo. (*dim.*)
Dotted Half Note	A note three beats long in duration. (𝅗𝅥.) A dot adds half the value of the original note.
Double Bar (𝄁)	Indicates the end of a piece of music.
Down Bow (⊓)	Drawing the bow downward, towards the floor.
Duet	A composition with two different parts played together.
Dynamics	Dynamics indicate how loud or soft to play a passage of music.
Eighth Note	An Eighth Note (♪) receives half the value of a quarter note, that is, half a beat. Two or more eighth notes are usually joined together with a beam, as follows: ♫
Eighth Rest	Indicates 1/2 beat of silence. (𝄾)
Enharmonics	Two notes that are written differently, but sound the same (and played with the same fingering) are called Enharmonics (F♯ and G♭).

Fermata	The Fermata (⌢) indicates that a note (or rest) is held somewhat longer than normal.
Flat (♭)	Lowers the note a half step and remains in effect for the entire measure.
Forte (𝆑)	Play loudly.
Half Note	A Half Note (𝅗𝅥) receives two beats. It's equal in length to two quarter notes.
Half Rest	The Half Rest (▬) marks two beats of silence.
Harmony	Two or more notes played together.
Interval	The distance between two pitches.
Key Signature	A Key Signature (the group of sharps or flats before the time signature) tells which notes are played as sharps or flats throughout the entire piece.
Largo	A very slow tempo.
Ledger Lines	Ledger Lines extend the music staff. Notes on ledger lines can be above or below the staff.
Mezzo Forte (𝐦𝆑)	Moderately loud.
Mezzo Piano (𝐦𝐩)	Moderately soft.
Moderato	Medium or moderate tempo.
Music Staff	The Music Staff has 5 lines and 4 spaces where notes and rests are written.
Natural Sign (♮)	Cancels a flat ♭ or sharp ♯ and remains in effect for the entire measure.
Notes	Notes tell us how high or low to play by their placement on a line or space of the music staff, and how long to play.
Phrase	A Phrase is a musical "sentence," often 2 or 4 measures long.
Piano (𝐩)	Soft.
Pitch	The highness or lowness of a note which is indicated by the horizontal placement of the note on the music staff.
Pick-Up Notes	One or more notes that come before the first full measure. The beats of Pick-Up Notes are subtracted from the last measure—also called "upbeats."
Pizzicato	Plucked.
Quarter Note	A Quarter Note (♩) receives one beat. There are 4 quarter notes in a $\frac{4}{4}$ measure.
Quarter Rest	The Quarter Rest (𝄽) marks one beat of silence.
Repeat Sign	The Repeat Sign means to play once again from the beginning without pause. Also, repeat the sections of music enclosed by the repeat signs ( ).

Rests	Beats of silence.
Rhythm	Rhythm refers to time—how long, or for how many beats a note lasts, including rests.
Scale	A sequence of notes in ascending or descending order. Like a musical "ladder," each step is the next consecutive note in the musical alphabet.
Sharp (♯)	Raises the note a half step and remains in effect for the entire measure.
Slur	A curved line connecting notes of different pitch.
Tempo	The speed of music.
Tie	A curved line connecting two notes of the same pitch. A tie between two notes makes the first note last the value of both notes "tied" together.
Time Signature	Indicates how many beats per measure and what kind of note gets one beat.
Treble Clef (𝄞)	(G Clef) indicates the position of note names on a music staff: The second line in Treble Clef is G.
Up Bow (V)	Drawing the bow upward, towards you.
Upbeat	See "pick-up note."
Whole Note	A Whole Note (𝅝) lasts for four full beats (a complete measure in $\frac{4}{4}$ time).
Whole Rest	The Whole Rest (▬) indicates a whole measure of silence.